The True Adventures of a Great Blue Heron

by Melissa L. Peebles

First edition November 2022
Interlachen, FL

Book design by Veronica Scott

Library of Congress Control Number: 2022916119
Published in the United States of America

ISBN 979-8-9866800-0-2 (hardcover)
ISBN 979-8-9866800-1-9 (paperback)
ISBN 979-8-9866800-2-6 (ebook)

Find me on Facebook!

https://www.facebook.com/LarryBird.TheTrueAdventuresofaGreatBlueHeron

This story is dedicated to Larry Bird!
From the family that has loved him for 16 years.

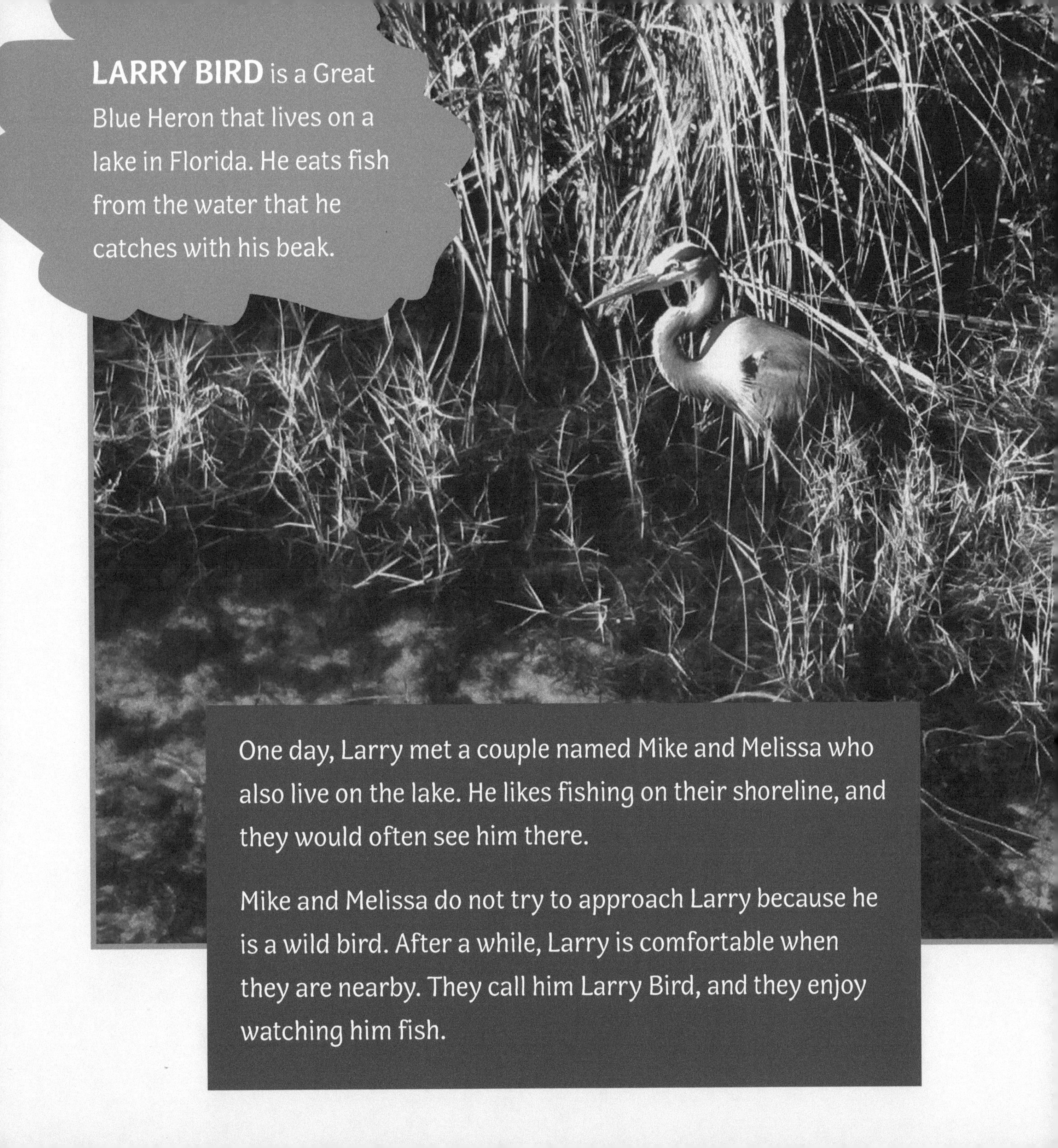

LARRY BIRD is a Great Blue Heron that lives on a lake in Florida. He eats fish from the water that he catches with his beak.

One day, Larry met a couple named Mike and Melissa who also live on the lake. He likes fishing on their shoreline, and they would often see him there.

Mike and Melissa do not try to approach Larry because he is a wild bird. After a while, Larry is comfortable when they are nearby. They call him Larry Bird, and they enjoy watching him fish.

Larry Bird also likes resting on their dock in the sunshine. Sometimes, Mike and Melissa have family and friends who visit. At first, Larry was timid. But soon, he felt at ease with visitors. They all like it when Larry comes to see them!

The family usually brings their children and their dogs with them to visit.

Larry Bird likes children as long as no one gets too close to him, but he is afraid of dogs. Larry flies to the roof of the dock to be away from the dogs, and still be near the family.

One day, Larry Bird got a fishing hook in his leg! Larry couldn't get the hook out, and he limped terribly when he tried to walk or fish. Melissa saw that Larry was hurt, and could not fish on his own. She knew he must be getting very hungry!

Mike and Melissa could not touch Larry Bird to remove the hook, because he would be afraid. Melissa worried that Larry would not be able to catch anything to eat until his leg healed, so she caught a fish and threw it on the shore for Larry Bird. He got very excited, and he ate the fish!

Now, Larry Bird is not afraid to get even closer to the family! They still never try to touch him, but Mike or Melissa caught a fish for Larry to eat every day, until his leg was better.

After a while, the fishing hook rusted away. Larry Bird's leg healed, and he could fish again! However, he was a little out of practice, and he liked it when the family would catch a fish for him.

Melissa knew that Larry had to fish on his own, so she threw fish food into the water to attract the fish closer to the shore. Larry Bird got excited when he saw the fish, and he caught one!

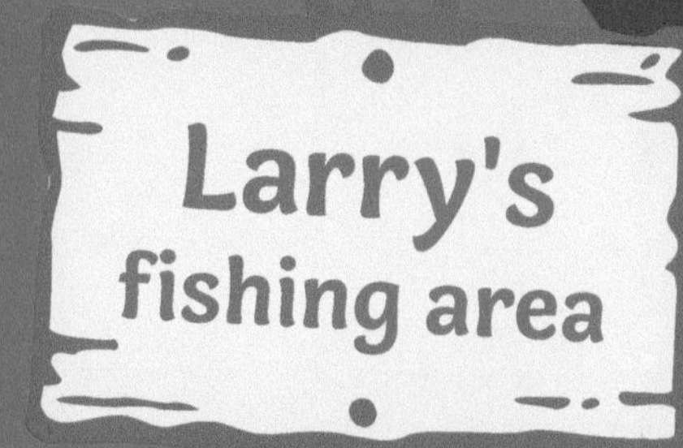

Then, even though Larry Bird was better, he still visits almost every day!

He fishes along the shoreline again, but he also wants Mike or Melissa to throw the fish food, so he can catch a fish easier!

They throw the fish food so Larry Bird can fish from the dock, or the dock steps. Deeper water means a bigger fish for Larry, and he likes bigger fish!
Larry Bird crouches, so the fish cannot see him. This is Larry's fishing stance.

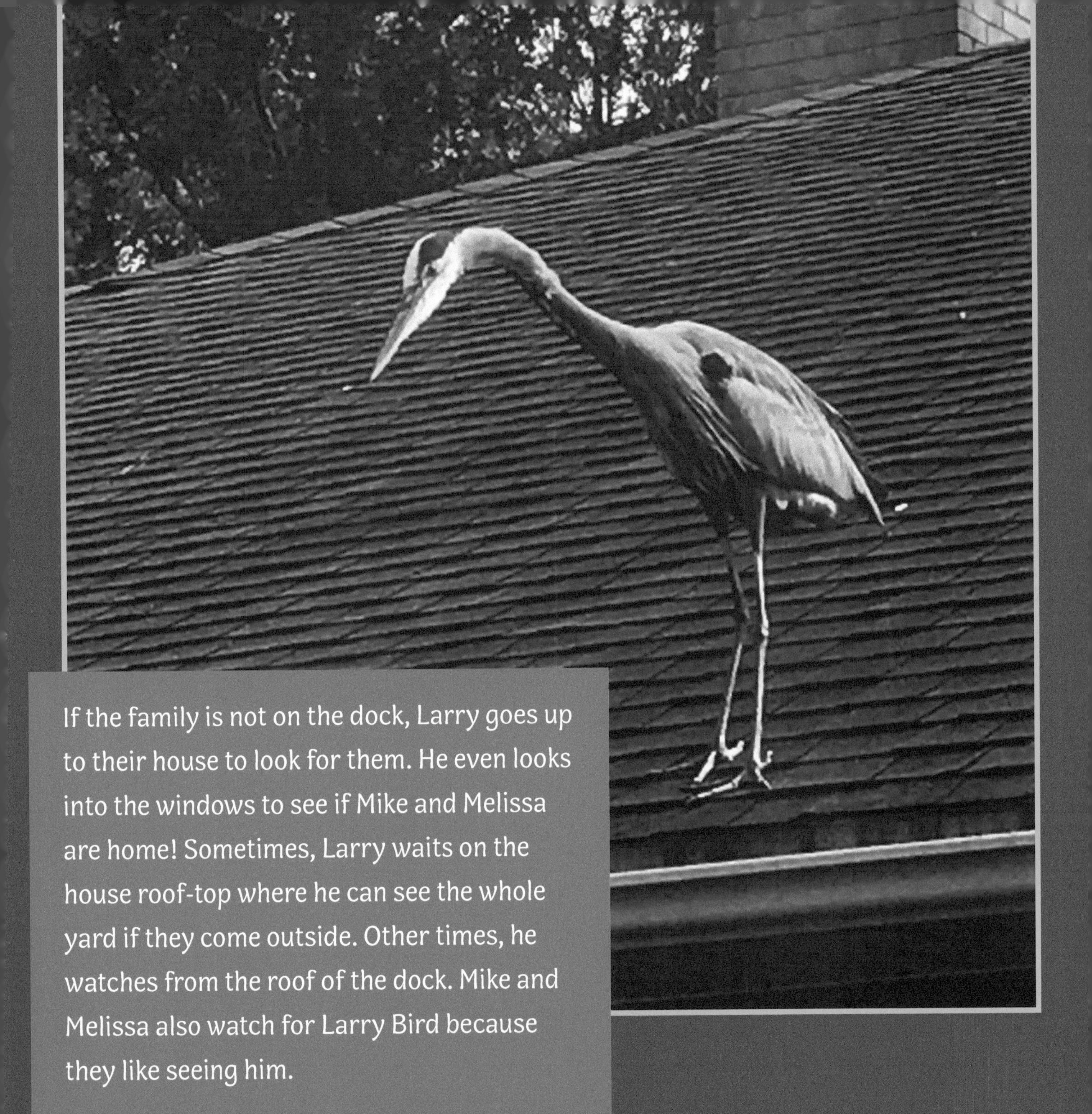

If the family is not on the dock, Larry goes up to their house to look for them. He even looks into the windows to see if Mike and Melissa are home! Sometimes, Larry waits on the house roof-top where he can see the whole yard if they come outside. Other times, he watches from the roof of the dock. Mike and Melissa also watch for Larry Bird because they like seeing him.

One time, Larry Bird even followed Mike and Melissa across the street to a neighbor's house!

In winter, occasionally it gets very cold and the fish swim to deeper water to be warmer. Then, there are no fish near the shore or dock for Larry Bird to catch! If this happens, Melissa goes to the fishing bait store and buys a fish for him to eat until the fish in the lake return.

One day, Larry was fishing from the dock steps and one of his feet became wedged between the steps. Larry was very upset!

Melissa wanted to help him, but Larry was frightened. He flapped his large wings until his foot was free, and flew away.

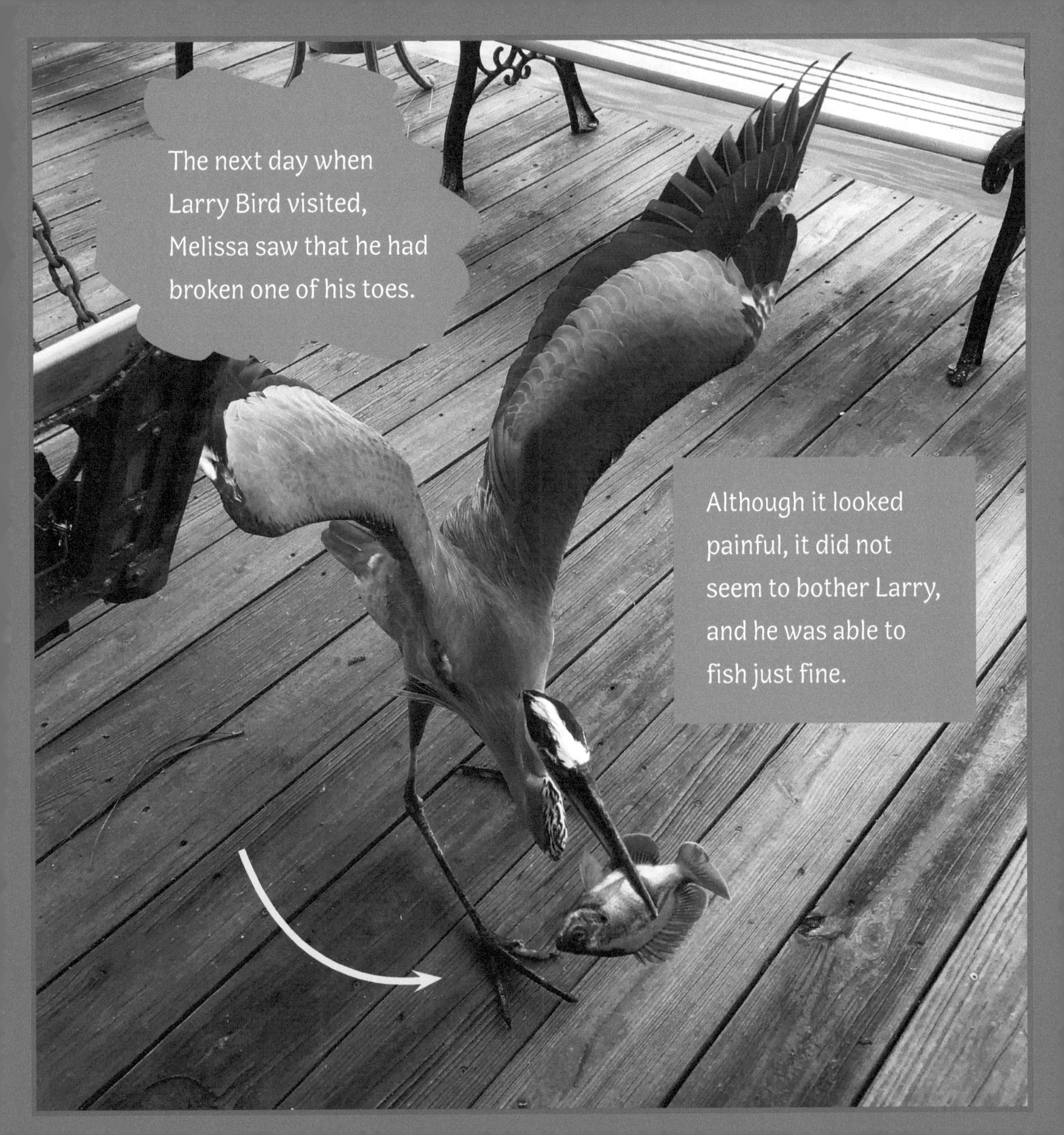
The next day when Larry Bird visited, Melissa saw that he had broken one of his toes.
Although it looked painful, it did not seem to bother Larry, and he was able to fish just fine.

With a little time, Larry Bird's broken toe fell off. There was a small stump where it had been.

Now, Mike and Melissa can recognize Larry from any other Great Blue Heron because his foot is different from theirs.

Larry Bird
occasionally
takes a bath
in the lake, but
most of the time
he opens his wings
to sunbathe.

The sunlight helps
Larry to preen, or
remove parasites and
dirt from his feathers with
his beak. Larry likes to have
clean feathers!

Even though Larry cleans his feathers often, sometimes he still gets an itch and has to scratch it! The family thinks Larry looks funny when he scratches!

Sometimes, Florida has big storms, or even a hurricane. Larry Bird lives outside, so he gets very wet! The family worries for Larry until they see him again.

They are always happy to see that he is safe after bad weather. Even if he looks like this!

Thankfully, it doesn't take long for Larry Bird to dry. With a little preening of his feathers, he is fluffed up and beautiful again!

One year, there was so much rain that the dock was flooded from the lake water rising. This did not bother Larry Bird. He doesn't mind getting his feet wet, and he still visits Mike and Melissa on the dock.

Larry Bird sometimes stays with Melissa until sunset. After dark, Larry likes to roost in a tall tree to be safe from predators.

Mike and Melissa, and their family, have been friends with Larry for many years. The family loves Larry Bird, and they believe he loves them too!
Larry Bird waves Goodbye!

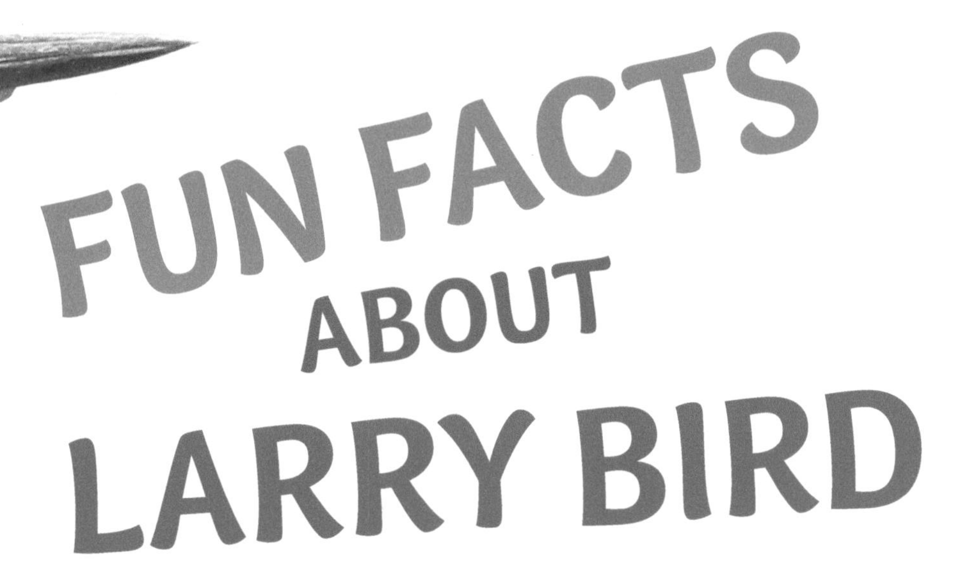

FUN FACTS ABOUT LARRY BIRD

Larry Bird is a **GREAT BLUE HERON** and he is the largest in the heron family. He can be **4 FEET TALL** when his neck is stretched up, with a wingspan of **6 FEET**.

Larry is a **WADING BIRD**. He has long thin legs for wading in shallow water to quietly and patiently search for his food. He also has a **LONG NECK** and a sharp beak for striking very fast, even under the water.

Although Larry Bird lives on a **FRESHWATER** lake in Florida, Great Blue Herons can live **ALL ACROSS NORTH AMERICA**, near fresh water or salt water.

Some Great Blue Herons in the north **MIGRATE SOUTH** for the winter, but those that live in the south like Larry Bird can stay **YEAR ROUND**.

Although **LARRY** is a big bird, he only weighs about **5 POUNDS**. This is because he has **HOLLOW BONES** to be lightweight for flying.

Larry eats mostly **FISH**, but he will also eat other things like **INSECTS, FROGS, LIZARDS**, and small mammals like **MICE**. He can swallow food **MUCH LARGER** than his narrow neck.

Larry Bird's call is a **DEEP AND HOARSE CROAKING** or **SQUAWK**, but he can make other quieter sounds too.

Larry flies with his **NECK TUCKED** in an S shape and his legs straight out behind him. His large wings flap slowly, but he can fly **20 TO 30 MILES PER HOUR**.

On hot days, Larry might have his wings **OPEN** and **DROOPED**, with an open beak and his neck muscles fluttering. This is a bird's way of **PANTING TO KEEP COOLER**.

Great Blue Herons normally **LIVE ALONE** and protect their territory. But in mating season, they like to **NEST IN A GROUP** or colony. They build large nests in the tallest trees, near or over water for **ADDED PROTECTION** and **FOOD SUPPLY**.

ABOUT THE AUTHOR

Melissa is a lover of nature, animals and wildlife! She is an avid hiker of forests and parks, and especially fond of exploring new places. Sometimes, she even likes to fly like Larry Bird!

Also enjoying water sports such as swimming, boating and kayaking, she and her husband made their family home on a lake in Florida.

It was here that her affectionate relationship with a wild Great Blue Heron over many years, and a unique opportunity for photos, inspired her to write a book to share their story.

CPSIA information can be obtained
at www.ICGtesting.com
Printed in the USA
LVHW070355121022
730467LV00009B/184